the berry
takes the shape
of the bloom

ALSO BY ANDREA BENNETT

Canoodlers

*Like a Boy but Not a Boy: Navigating Life, Mental
Health, and Parenthood outside the Gender Binary*

Moon Montréal

Moon Québec City

the berry
takes the shape
of the bloom

poems

andrea bennett

Talonbooks

Talonbooks
9259 Shaughnessy Street, Vancouver, British Columbia, Canada v6p 6r4
talonbooks.com

Talonbooks is located on xʷməθkʷəy̓əm, Sḵwx̱wú7mesh, and səlilwətał Lands.

First printing: 2023

Typeset in Jenson
Printed and bound in Canada on 100% post-consumer recycled paper

Interior design by Typesmith
Cover embroidery by andrea bennett
Cover design by andrea bennett and Typesmith

Talonbooks acknowledges the financial support of the Canada Council for the Arts, the Government of Canada through the Canada Book Fund, and the Province of British Columbia through the British Columbia Arts Council and the Book Publishing Tax Credit.

Library and Archives Canada Cataloguing in Publication

Title: The berry takes the shape of the bloom : poems / Andrea Bennett.
Names: bennett, andrea (Author of Canoodlers), author.
Identifiers: Canadiana 20230169414 | isbn 9781772015515 (softcover)
Classification: lcc ps8603.e5593 c35 2023 | ddc c811/.6—dc23

For Sinclair

Desires as round as peaches
bloom in me all night.

—ANNE CARSON
Short Talks (1992)

The head of a pineapple turns into its
offspring's base, leaves a commitment to the
golden flesh to follow. I visit my friend in
Australia, and we take a little train through
a field, past rows of pineapples growing;
kangaroos, wallabies, a local goanna who
chooses to live in the zoo. After the train, I take
a picture of my friend and her family: three
generations posed in front of a giant spiky fruit.

Turn water to milk. Turn coffee, turn cider,
turn Diet Coke to milk. Turn pretzels, turn
cheese, turn pizza, turn carrots, turn miso.
Turn another's milk to milk. Turn everything,
turn the whole wide world, to milk.

The transsexual empire has been coming like
the Apocalypse, forever and very soon. Every
time I command the empire it becomes a
warrenful of rabbits late for a party. We are
never on time. We are too soon and no longer
on trend. I dreamed that the only way to get
to a party was to take the carnival swings and
I kept falling off. I heard that we enforced the
binary by being nonbinary. *Look!* The fear said
as it plundered. *Over there! An empire.*

My maternal family slides off into the ocean and
resurfaces from time to time, sleek as a harbour
seal. They want me to love my mother   but
I nothing my mother. I want them to love me
and they want me to love my mother.

It makes me want to die and it makes me want
to live forever and I understand, for the first
time, why it is my mother buries herself every
night. Buries herself   until morning comes.
Buries herself so there's a self left to unearth.

When people said *stay hungry* I thought they meant it literally, stay hungry because that was the price of being thin. When they said *salad days* I thought it meant the days when we were young enough to be always hungry and only eating salad. I can tell you how many calories are in an apple and how many calories make up a pound. I can tell you how many pounds my mother weighs and how old I was when I surpassed her weight. The only time I was thin the thinness came because I was sick and couldn't eat. When the sickness lifted I felt relief and sadness. When people say *unhealthy* they mean fat. When people say *unhealthy* they do not mean what *unhealthy* has done to my brain.

I would find it comforting. I understand it's selfish. But I wish the dead *would* haunt the living.

An ex once sent me flowers after I'd decided to leave him. Blooms and a note in a glass vase. They could have been tulips; they could have been chrysanthemums. What I remember with clarity is the dread of watching them wilt towards their inevitable home in the compost. Knowing I'd let their immersed stems turn slick, begin to melt into vegetal slime, because it's hard to say goodbye to a thing that was once living. Later I'd learn to like lilies: their insistent scent, their stamens staining all they touch.

As a child I pictured all the different ways I could be alone. Whatever cake I would make would last as long as I wanted it to and my entire household would know my favourite things because I would be my entire household. Not a thread out of place on the area rug. A whole wall full of books. Always a pineapple on the kitchen counter. When nobody loves your unruly body it is hard to believe that anyone ever would. That you could   trust them to. As a child I believed that solitude was a promise I could keep.

I had a temper so hot it could fry an egg. Like a
key breaking off inside a rusted U-lock. Like an
unanchored bookshelf in an earthquake. Like a
crow picking a fight with an eagle.

        I had a temper so hot the
woods got lost in me. Like a jawbreaker looking
for fillings. I swallowed the key, I swallowed the
books, I swallowed the lock and the crow and the
earthquake. I swallowed it all and I was still hungry.

My favourite ex forgot I'd told him I was leaving
the party. He ran the streets of the Ward, in
Guelph, to find me and make sure I was safe. He
was drunk and when he found me I was mad.
I said *I told you*, and his worry turned to anger.
He called me things my mother had, said all
the things about myself I secretly knew to be
true. We argued in the street and then he left
again and I was alone. I lit a cigarette, smoked
it, stubbed it out on the muscled, rounded flesh
of my calf. I had nice calves and I wanted them
to burn. Like saying   *here, let me, I will do
it for you*, or like saying *nothing you can do will
hold a candle*. By the time the leg healed he was
sleeping on the floor in the other bedroom. He
slept with a friend of ours in there, and then years
later I visited them and stayed on their couch. I
liked her, I liked them, I wanted it all to work out.

My neighbour's magnolia is one thousand birds
in the early stages of flight. I would gently cup
a blossom and wait. I am getting groceries, or
late for preschool pickup. The rabbit   is
tapping his watch. The time I take comes later,
before sleep, when the birds visit me as I am
thinking of the dead.

Sinclair is learning subject–verb agreement.
She takes the bookmark from *How to Write
an Autobiographical Novel*, which I've been
reading for too long a portion of her life. I keep
returning to an essay about a rose garden, the
idea that helping something flourish could keep
me alive. I love the way Sinclair sits on her push
bike—looking, watching, her boots pulling
her across the wood-chip paths of the garden.
She eats the growing tip from a pea shoot; she
pinches off a set of mint leaves, puts them in
her mouth directly, aphids and all.

In the overlap between the lupin blooming and the peas forming pods, we eat three cantaloupes from the grocery store, and Mexico before that.

I like the moment in his TV show after Jamie Oliver shows American children how their chicken nuggets are made. *Some of the processed foods you love are made from the bits you don't like,* he says, blending up a carcass as they *eeeeeeee*. It's a test. Post blending, he asks *who would still eat this?* as their little American hands shoot up like sunflowers.

Nose-to-tail eating, I think, every time I return to the clip. The hubris of someone wanting to teach us why we're all so stupid.

The time the melons spend on the vine; the time that people spend seeding them and planting them out and picking them. The melons landing in waxed paper boxes, the time they spend in there, on the truck. And my six melons, one felled by slugs in its sixth week of life. Organic and growing up a trellis made of laurel branches. I will eat both kinds of melon and be grateful.

I receive a picture of blooms from a family
member in the desert. I don't always remember
who I've been family to. I don't know what I've
felt. Tomorrow I will remember and the force
of remembering will make me forget again. I
am rich like poundcake with family. I am an
airy crumb   where the family used to go. ·

Greenwich Mean Time −2 is promising. On
this map, a strip of pinkish-red stretching
north and south. Skipping Kalaallit Nunaat
(Greenland) at −3, unfurling along the North
Atlantic past Iceland, the Azores. In Brazil, it
takes Saint Peter and Saint Paul, Trindade and
Martim Vaz. And then finally South Georgia
and South Sandwich. In the end, not the
place to share a time zone with no land mass,
only other boats and whales and turtles and
whatever else finds its place in the mercy of the
sea. Not a place to be as completely alone as a
person sometimes feels.

I dream I'm looking for my cat, who's not inside
or on the balcony. In the alley, another tabby,
not her. A black cat, a longhair, a tortie. Not
her. An email someone sends to me mistakenly
reads *"Keeping Secrets" has since been taken
elsewhere.*

I want to feel the urgent relief of seeing her face
among all the other alley-cat faces. I look and
look and never see her face.

A poem for the ginger tea I let steep too long,
until each sip was a rebuke. One for the woman
working at the grocery store, with a headache,
behind the useless piece of Plexiglas beaming
a glint of light directly at her dominant eye.
Another for the serrated tomia of geese. One
for the audience member fuming about *theydies*.
A poem for the Walla Walla onion seedlings the
bear crushed two days after we planted them
out. Poems like so many all-seeing eyes, poems
witnessing, poems like a parent or a cousin, a
friend you can call for a hug and some solace.

A friend writes about breasts and dysphoria.
Apart from her, around me like a hula hoop,
one thought tumbles after the other: I'll never
prioritize what it feels like to look at my body
over what it feels like to be in my body, I'll never
be able to prioritize what it feels like to look at
my body over what it feels like to be in my body.
My body will never look like a man's because
I've internalized what men are supposed to do
with their appetites: satiate them.

I poemed my breasts once or twice; read the
poems aloud, felt naked in public.

It took us three tries before we found a shower
curtain for our new place. We used a tape
measure but the packages lied: too short, too
short, okay. We settled on peacocks and paisley, a
busy bacchanalia in creams, yellows, and browns.

My mother's love missed me like an arrow misses
a deer. I am several ghosts. I paisley-curve my
shoulders around the cream of my legible chest.
I bear my poems. I bear my hooves.

It takes me three tries to tell him: I don't want to
be haunted, not anymore. I would like to strike
this stanza, ball it up and start over.

As the summer breaks, I collect five new things
to wake me in the middle of the night. Some
floods will brook rain boots and others need
boats. You can do the right right right thing
and end up travelling in the same direction. You
can convince yourself: *I am buoyant* but forget
about sewage and currents.

We bring the cat to Al Purdy's A-frame and she
keens in front of the picture window. Later her
tail shakes and she is happy. She lifts her paw
above a fat ant and doesn't strike. She circles the
perimeter. She circles nose to tail on the couch
and settles beside Will, who is napping.

Next door there is a heron and a heron
simulacrum. The dummy faces, always,
northeast. The other cranes its neck, straightens,
swivels like a periscope. It stays all morning,
the cat watching out the window, and then flies
away, its neck bulging like the skin of her belly.

I made my first chapbook the week my
gallbladder came out: bad poetry, photocopies,
fabrics—a shot of my friend riding U of G's
cannon transposed over the faces of canonical
CanLit. I took sick leave from a communications
job; before that, I lived in the library. (I used to ·
bike books over to my professor's house, drink
her Turkish coffee.) At twenty-three I thought
heartburn was something I'd earned—too fat,
too sad, too many jobs. At thirty-two I learn the
fetus has grown to the size of a lime, and ask
Will to buy antacids while he's out.

Ten weeks: a nurse weighs me and takes my
blood pressure, and then I am half-bare in
stirrups, with Will in the room. Before we go,
blue gel on my stomach, a small machine—we
see a series of circles, and wait, and wait. Finally,
the doctor says *you hear it? The heartbeat.*

Eleven weeks: the fetus is the size of a fig. I can
grow without the fetus but the fetus needs me.
(I picture Will and me and a baby at a picnic in
the park, on a blanket; she looks up at a robin and
laughs.) My mood grows grey housing the fetus—
not because of, but because of the fetus. Because of
my body remaking itself as a vessel. The afternoons
are the hardest: I cry a small child's despair every
day at 3 p.m. I hope this fig grows and grows and
is fine and healthy. I hope this for the fig and for
myself, so I only need to grow her once.

On the métro I read a longform piece about warehouse
workers: this labour separates the wheat from the
chaff. The chaff dwindle and drop in the aisles, holding
scanners, utilitarian shoes perpendicular to the floor.
Some of us have professions, while others have two
degrees and three jobs. Last Christmas I was alone at
a writing retreat and this Christmas I am restocking
endcaps on overnight shifts—remarkable for its
normalcy. Remember how we pressed our temples
in the nineties: we have *too* much, we have too *much*.
True and   not true. Anyone who can has been
feasting on roasted piglets for years, and the rest of us
are wondering where all the full-grown pigs have gone.

My mood is the flap-flap-dip of a bird's
flight. My tastes have reverted to comfort
food—beans on toast, cheese slices, ants on
a log. Slivered raw onions on a plain hot dog
with ketchup. The day is long and cool and
punctuated by meals, sleep, hummingbirds,
and herons. Ants carrying their dead across
the living room floor. Out of habit, more than
mourning: the bodies will be heaped onto the
midden with whatever else is no longer needed.

Each week, the embryo I've been carrying is likened to food: sesame seed, chickpea, kidney bean. Relatable, like the koan. *There is no such thing as being a little bit pregnant.*

Only, this is what it's felt like. Two pink lines with a promise that could fade, like wax crayon preventing dye on the shell of an Easter egg. *I'm pregnant,* I tell my practical friend. *I'm pregnant,* I tell my friend who will have two under two, *but I might not stay that way.*

The place where I get my hair cut is chockablock with young trans parents. It's not time to worry yet about how I'll ask not to be called *mom.* First, *madame* has appointments, ultrasounds, preventative healthcare for the at-risk postpartum period, no energy left over to say *I'm not her.*

When Will comes to the A-frame, he unplugs
everything that makes noise. The mouse
deterrent, the mid-century modern clock. He
asks why it doesn't bother me.

I live in one corner of my body at a time, hidden
from the part that hears the high-pitched
whine, the off-rhythm clack of the minute hand.
(A mouse came despite the mouse deterrent:
round little eyes, round little ears, short little
snout. We saw each other and the time when
I could have done anything clack-clacked past.
I shut the cupboard and went back to bed.)

The moon is on course to blot out the sun. The planetarium holds a viewing party, free, a quick walk from Pie-IX station on the Green line. When I open my planner the Monday of, the note is an admonition: every once in a while a total eclipse, but today and every day a deadline.

Will and I watch the Vancouver episode of *Art in the Twenty-First Century* and a woman who makes art for condos says, pouring plaster into a glove mould, *some people stop living before they die.* She says *the real question is, is there life before death?* My laptop, overheated, shuts itself off.

In the fall of 1999, at the age of thirty-five, Ann
Patchett gets the chicken pox. And then an
intermittent case of idiopathic hives. Her friend
Lucy suggests she document them. Face swollen
shut, face open; ankles the size of grapefruits
and, then again, thin and sleek.

In the fall of 2017, at thirty-three or thirty-four
weeks pregnant, an itch begins at my ankles and
builds. We're sent for an ultrasound and I cry
on the table, head upstairs to triage. In *Truth
and Beauty*, Lucy is the kind of sick that leads to
dying, and Ann the kind where you are mostly
fine. I haven't slept in days but it's just an itch.
Upstairs, the nurses are so kind. They perform a
little bloodletting, *une prise de sang*, the internal
made external. A preview of what is to come.
The baby is small, the baby is breech; in the end,
the itching is idiopathic. I am so tired, I am so
lucky—*why I am not sharing my largesse*—I am
so lucky. On the monitor, her heartbeat marches
forward; we are fine for now, for now, for now.

I take a break at Christmas to observe another
family's traditions; I find an old journal in the tool
closet and remember the smell of rabbit hutches
and one-hitters full of resin; I go to the boat spa
and let myself fill with steam scented like mint and
cardamom and eucalyptus and oranges; I swim
and swim and then lie on my back, floating, eyes
closed, trusting I won't drift too far.

Bell pepper, half a footlong, a small cantaloupe.
My friend dies two months after he told me
his wife was expecting, the same day I go for
my second ultrasound. *Why.*   I read and
reread the last email he sent me: it is as if part
of him lives on in little bundles he gifted before
he left. I see the fetus squirming and kicking
onscreen. She is hale and hearty, shows us her
fists and feet. She is making her way through
the produce stand. We are okay for no reason.
(He should have grown old.)

Every year a year further from the time before I
existed, a year closer to the time I'll no longer exist.

The fetus isn't upside down, as she's supposed to be.
She's sunny side up and wrong. Her head knocking at
my ribcage as if it might swing open onto the world.

The shock of winter takes the leaves from the trees
while they are still green. This time last year there
was no human-to-be. This time this year she is and
she is not. She may turn. She may shock to the
world, still green.

There will be setting the alarm for midnight to
feed the baby. The rattle of the coat hook on the
door as I close it against the cat. Sneezing again
and again, the rasp of toilet paper against my raw,
red nostrils. Pumping milk and milk and milk.
The feeling of being half a compound noun. The
cat against the door. The dull sinus headache of
another man hiding behind some woman like
she is curtains or his mother's long skirt. Maybe
I shouldn't tug on the owl at the corner of my
consciousness worrying about violence and dying.
I will open the window a crack when I use the gas
oven. Wet a cloth, dab the baby, hold the baby.

Any girl-boy who's too big for their
britches. Any boy who's made herself
wholer by leaving things behind. Any
holier boy. Any supporting role. Any hole
where the old family used to go. Holler.

I look up at the sky and think of burned
marshmallows, sweet and acrid, smelling of
fire. On earth, *grossesse*: watching a pot to see
if the kernel will pop. The watcher, the vessel,
the watched. Two bodies, one visible. I flip my
hands in and out like paddles, saying *she kicks!*
A friend with a newborn writes, after speaking
of birth, *I'm sorry if I scared you.*

Will and I and the cat are watching TV when
the cat jumps down from the couch and looks
for a minute like a Holland lop I knew once.
Suddenly I am in 2008 Guelph and not 2017
Montréal, the old apartment, seeing Acorn's
tawny haunches hop away from me. I ask Will
if he ever experiences vertigo but for time—*do
the planes of your world ever collapse?*

He says no, they don't.

Maybe in my inbox. Maybe through the mail. Maybe hiding in my spam folder. A thing, something big. Something big that will solve it forever and for good.

Six adult geese, a honking cluster of goslings. Grooming themselves while a grackle looks on from the bough of a cedar. The beaks of the geese plunge towards their breasts and wing feathers until their necks look like question marks. I watch from the deck and they take turns watching me.

June bugs, like sentient blimps, ricochet off the picture window. It will rain every day until it stops. I am the rusty bike leaned up for shelter against the house.

When she was young, a man installed
an oblivion button somewhere between my
mother's throat and her heart. When I was
young, she did the same   for me.

Dicing carrots, I argue with
                              the idea of her. She
talks in platitudes but is cowed in my kitchen.
The kitchen knife comes with a sheath; I build
a safety guard for the button.

(I can knock that guard up with my index
finger, take a breath, press *fuck it*.)

In the fall I do not know how to ask for what I
want because I do not know what I want. The
baby-measuring produce has diverged paths.
My belly has grown too big for biking. I am
standing on the ledge of a cataract of tears
that will not come. I say *I can't do this*. I feel
the baby kick, punch; the cat lets me hug her.
Too far and too soon. *What if it's always like
this*. A tearless cataract is just a cliff. A cabbage
could be big or small. No one can think about a
coconut without seeing it shatter.

As a child, I dreamed a stone fountain carved
into the shape of a bear on its hind legs came
to life and chased my picnicking family. In my
twenties, a log broke free from an 18-wheeler and
came through our windshield. Just last night, a
thundercloud of gunpowder rained down from
the sky. My friend and I took shelter inside the car
she drove throughout high school; my ultrasound
was bumped in favour of tending to the wounded.

I pray the bike mechanic's prayer over the truing
stand, balancing the needs of the radial and the
lateral. My psalms for hubs, when overhauled,
that feel like butter. The pulpit of flat fixes. The
way I know my customers first by their bikes.
The raiment of Park Tool. The sacrament of
lemon-yellow degreaser. The pre-rounding give
of a spoke nipple the closest I'll come to hearing
a sacred object's voice—*what is your will for me?*

When I was nine, we went to Jamaica, where my grandfather's family lived in the hills. We stayed in one fancy hotel, and then another. A hurricane drew shut the curtains of the sky. We ate fried plantain, pineapple; drank soursop juice. I stayed in the pool until I was called out. Swam up to the bar and asked again and again for virgin daiquiris, until my mother said *not that word!* and I burned with the shame of implying sex. I had developed breasts too early and shame too late. The rains fell.

Gone are the days of dawdling down in my granddad's garden. The year the asparagus bolted and the summer squash bulged with rain. Gone are the days I thought I'd run out of things to say about my mother.

My nana said *I don't know why people have Facebook*. My nana meant *please stop writing about the family*.

That year the zucchini grew too big for their britches, I smashed one between stones in the corner of the yard. *You know your mother loves you more than anything*.

Gone are the days of waiting to see what the clouds will bring. I hold the pressure. I hold two fronts. I held the rain until I couldn't.

Will's friend says of Sinclair *everything about her is round*. My father's father had the roundest face; he gave my dad his name and not much else. I got the roundness and the name and I passed them on. My father's father died before Sinclair was born but we didn't find out until much later.

In my twenties I listened to *Coast to Coast* AM
with George Noory with my ex, who smuggled
mickeys into work. I am no longer in my youth.
There is a latitude we extend to children that
I didn't want to extend to adults. But there we
were, smuggling mickeys and talking about
energy vampires. My ex used boxes covered
with thrifted silk scarves for furniture. He made
eye contact with a cop and took the longest
drag of his joint that he could. That wasn't what
I wanted. After I left I hoped he'd get sober.
After I left I learned how to stop wanting things
for people that they don't want for themselves.

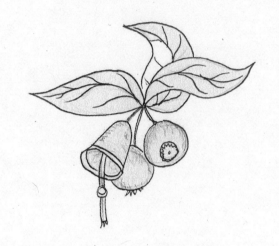

As common as bladderwrack and not quite attractive enough to be an underdog in the imaginary autobiography of my own life. Every time I enter the ocean, through its eelgrass, between its moon jellies, I take a little bit home with me. It is fine to be common. It is a gift to enter the ocean on the same patch of intertidal sand, to take in its changes and its constancy, its cycles, its gossip, its anger, its gripes.

The arched back of audible tension in a horror
film. At night, in bed, when I've placed my
phone face down and closed my eyes against
the fear it will be the last time I close them,
I am Drew Barrymore at the beginning of
Scream, making foiled camping popcorn on
the stove. I am the replaceable youth whose
T-top ran out of gas in a rural area. "Tinnitus"
suggests metal, which suits: a hot, bloody
iron taste at the sides of the tongue. The call
coming, unanswered, from inside the house.

On the way to his sister's bridal shower, Will
and I stop for limeade. (Margaritas are the
maternal drink of his family.) In line, hands on
the sweating cardboard, I think of an ex with a
troubled present: *is he still alive?*

I still remember my ex's PIN, I confess in the
parking lot. Will ducks his shoulder, and then
his head, into the driver's side of the car. *Do you
still remember his credit card number?*

Like it's *The Last Picture Show* and someone is
documenting our momentous lives, a bare-bones
grandfather turns his desert Jeep into the lot
ahead of us, and three motorcycles cruise by:
doppler bluegrass.

On the highway, a deer paints the road red as
if smeared crosswise by a giant thumb. Further
south, the dotted centre line hacks up hawk
feathers. Gristle glues them to the pavement.
The wind exacts a waving, grim hello.

My dirtbag ex ran out of clay while crafting a
bust of his own head for a university class called
Sculpture I. He sat in front of a mirror and built
the clay up on a Styrofoam base until it began
to resemble him. By the time he got to his hair,
he was running low. He handed me a pair of
scissors. As the first curls fell, I understood the
intimacy of the barber. The moment passed.

I had to set it with curtains

                and close them when the
action wasn't the drama meant for the stage. We
set it in a place and made it universal. She set it in
a place and we performed the expected volume of
gratitude and laughter and tears.

We read the room. We read her   and we
read her room. We were polite   and our
faces thumb-licked for show. Backstage or with
the curtains drawn we were   a problem,
a big problem, a selfish   high-horse
problem, a problem so big it was only

                      a matter of time.

I tongued the street and it told me who'd died.
For those who weren't sick, I asked why or how,
as if knowing could make it reversible. A woman
walked here, and then she didn't anymore. That's
it. Justice is for the living. I tongued the street
again and heard a different language: a man who
died a living death. A man who was our friend
and then was not. We saw it but we didn't see it
well enough. He teetered down the curb and our
fingertips feathered him straight for a time.

I had another ex who said it was bad to drink
coffee from a straw—you could choose stained
teeth or you could choose cancer. We drank a lot
of coffee as I went briefly from myself to thin.
We jogged together. I met his parents and slept
on the basement couch in their home. Staring
at the ceiling, I thought *maybe I can make a run
for it.* I thought *I am not my best self   in
this relationship.* Later, I did make a run. Later, I
woke up gasping for air because he'd taken mine
once. Slowly I got to be myself again.

I learned how to braid on practice ice, skating
backwards c-cuts and crossovers around
the faceoff circles. Stick on the ice, not too
fast, each skater a strand. I would like to
know how to braid hair: fish or French or
in pigtails, falling neatly behind the ears. I
would like to braid myself into a lavender bath
and live there forever. I would like to make a
friendship bracelet out of bread—strand four
behind strand three, between strands one and
two, the generative promise of flour and yeast.

I want to be the fig and the wasp. A good tender
leaf. A worker. I listen for the two test kernels
to pop in the pot. My hearing is a peal of bells
that rings   and rings. I am sure the
kernels pop and pop but there they are, knees
tight to their chests. A bee goes by outside
and Sinclair tries to name it. She takes her
fingers out of her mouth and points. She can be
whatever she wants. I will buy her earplugs. I
want everyone to live forever. I want to give and
to take and maybe that's too much to want.

Separating the albumens from the yolks to
make *macarons*, I hesitate before classifying the
chalazae, the wound white strands holding the
yolk in place. If fatty, they will flatten the foam.
Before my grandma Garcia makes scrambled
eggs, she must remove them. Too reminiscent of
an umbilical cord, the connection between one
life and another. Today I am prudish, like I am
prudish when I refuse to eat an oyster, or a clam,
or an olive. With a spoon I edge each chalaza
from each white, separate it from the yolk, too.
Into the green bin, a shorter journey back to soil.

I teach Sinclair how to say hello to a dog. *Meow* she points. *He says "woof"* I say. *Can you say "woof"?* I hold my hand out to a terrier and receive a lick. *Hiiiii* she says. *Woo.* When you are a toddler, everything looks like the name of the first animal you learned. When you are a toddler, dogs are as tall or taller. When you are a toddler, *woof,* like *dog,* is sometimes a hair too close to wolf.

A poem for those of us who've thrown up into pull-tab bags on the Greyhound and held the vomit, warm and then cooling, until the next stop. Another for the man knee-deep in a city fountain in November, pulling oak and maple leaves from the drain. One for me: I dislocated my jaw while sleeping, and was not rewarded with the powers of a snake.

Together, we make an island loop. We rent a car and go looking for a forever home. Sinclair is beginning to notice where she ends and the world begins. We are learning a lesson: with object permanence comes the pain of loss.

The sun beats me out like a dusty rug. Will gives me his khaki bucket hat; my neck is so blistered I take it without asking *what about you?* No matter. He ties a scarf around his head and lets the ends hang down like an impromptu mullet.

The sand foreshortens my footstep. I get to leave no little boot tread here, no special memory of where I've stepped. All my water is gone now. I do not have the patience of a prickly pear. I am pink, I am plump, I am reddening. I am a kale plant ready to crop all winter before producing seeds.

The tenses of my favourite Ginsberg poem
suggest God gets in bed with man and wife. A
holy trinity. A holy lollipop that melts in the
mouth. God and man and wife, an eternal late-
fall morning, air chilled and skins clammy and
warm. A Day-Glo cabbage patch. Who knows
what's to come?

I'd like to have a body like a gun. Long and narrow, smooth and cold and steel, able to hold gunpowder. Instead I am soft like a cushion. I would like to be as taut as a wall. My pulp as protected as a tooth's. And yet my body insists. My body offers comfort, warmth, absorbs whatever an id has to spill.

To get the meat from the chicken, I start with a
knife, but it's so tender it cleaves from the bone
at my fingertips. I tell Will I don't know what I'm
doing. He says it's fine. My friend Ali used to say,
training people in the kitchen where we worked,
there is no right way.

In my first year of university I took mushrooms
and had a bad trip—something like a migraine
and the nadir of depression. I knew that part
would pass. But when I went to the bathroom to
drink from the tap, I saw and could not unsee the
scaffolding of skull under my face in the mirror.

One morning, leaning over my kitchen window,
holding a sponge to a plate, I watch two shirtless
men wrestle on a greying deck. They knock over
a patio table and everything is silent except for
their collisions and their breath. The smaller one
pins the larger one. They stay still for a moment,
tense. The pinned one takes his friend's face in
his hands, leans close   and whispers in his
ear; they break apart with a back slap, a teeter-
totter recentring.

I dreamed we abandoned our anxious life for a different one in Phoenix. I imagined a campus of new buildings, trying to look old. We lived together in a concrete single: one bed, two desks, and a hot plate. *Where is the library?* The dream was supposed to mean we could leave, but it also meant we would never start over. I palmed the concrete hallway and got stuck in its pores.

My mother haunts the margins of my life.
My mother said I *always*, I *never*, I *always*. My
mother got angry like the sky changes before
a summer storm. My mother bought clothing
four sizes too small for a daughter she didn't
have. My mother said *be grateful*. My mother
said *what you don't know*. My mother said I
was difficult. My mother said I was just like my
father. My mother slept with my best friend's
father, my mother said I couldn't stop working
at my best friend's father's store, my mother
slapped me across the face. My aunt said *please
stop writing about your mother* and the next day
I read aloud, at a festival, all the worst poems I'd
ever written about my mother.

Before blueberries grow, they grow a bloom that looks like a proto-berry. The berry then takes the shape of the bloom that came before it. The berry displaces the bloom that came before it. When people say that mothers and daughters have complicated relationships, what they mean is that the daughter is the blueberry and the mother is the bloom who came before it.

My mother bloomed   and then I was a wave or a skateboard or a foraging deer. My mother bloomed and I did not displace her in the right way. Did I berry? You can say that what you want is to hold a space that isn't fixed. You can say that's what you want but someone is always there to tell you the bloom is what comes before the berry.

I have a song stuck in my head. The horns repeat,
wending, like their shapes, through my dreams.
Sinclair stands with her toy guitar and watches
David Byrne on stage with St. Vincent. Byrne's
white hair, St. Vincent's blood-red lips. Byrne
bends his body; the child bends hers. St. Vincent
leans her body back, step-stepping her bare legs;
the child does the same. St. Vincent's lips stretch
back towards her cheekbones as she sings, like my
aunt's would if she still spoke to me. The horns
in my dreams remind me of the hunt. The child
is drawn to the horns and to Byrne at the side of
the stage, moving his body like a horn's human
incarnation. When the song ends and the band
says *thank you, thank you,* the child turns to the
audience in the living room and practises that, too.

Ten saffron crocuses wreath the garlic chives in
a knee-high cedar planter. In the fall I sink my
pinky two knuckles into mushroom compost for
each corm, which I mail-ordered online from a
store that also sells a book called *The Cannabis
Spa at Home*. The petals are to be purple: a watery,
striated wash of colour darker at the centre than
the tips. Each flower should produce three sunset-
orange stigmas, which I will pluck and dry, all
thirty together to make one golden-yellow pot
of rice. In late winter the corms' green tips begin
to break the surface of the soil. Soon their sharp,
grassy leaves look like upturned cocktail umbrellas.
Then an umbrella that has lost the ability to close:
yellowing and browning, slumped over as if having
lost the will to remain erect. In mid-May I water
them attentively but they are as unchanging as air
plants. I have to be faithful and wait. I have to be
patient and wait to see if they'll return in the fall.

As I grow older and develop a hint of jowl, the plump girl leaves my face. The first time I look in the mirror and see my whole self looking back, it is like leaving a steam room for the cold pinch of winter air.

In Montréal, Saint-Laurent is the dividing line between west and east. I walk it, up and down, and let the neighbourhoods change around me.

Today's mood is an overbleached kitchen
cloth Cintas should have retired several wash
cycles ago. It is nodding along as my therapist
talks about how hard the pandemic has been
for young moms with kids until I realize she's
mistaken me for a mom again. Today's fatigue
is the same as yesterday's: a raw feeling
around the eyes, raw like the way people
described my first book of poetry—genuine,
authentic. In Austen, for the wealthy: artless.
Today's mood is my cat on the deck, her little
breastbone perched at the edge of the deck,
meowing as I do squats with a resistance
band knotted around my thighs. Today's
mood is the marigolds I grow carelessly with
the tomatoes, the marigolds I grow because
my grandfather grew them with his tomatoes,
and I am so fond of him, even though the
fondness does not transfer to the marigolds.

The wildfire sun looks like a pearl
onion stuck in a jar of pickled beets.

I forget what poetics are. I forget the word for
the study of knowledge. I need a phrase when
the word is a thing unto itself, a special ornate
thing in itself. I work in the kitchen, where I
make the food. I work with the words as if they
are ripe tomatoes hot from a water bath, needing
to be skinned. Tomato tomato tomato over and
over, into the heat and with salt and a halved
onion and butter. I am sorry that I can't retain
the words I am supposed to know. I am too busy
having   personal news. I am a food mill and
poetics is a tomato skin. Sometimes I just want
to experience things as they are and be in my
body instead of thinking about things and my
body's relationship to them.

A girl's pants come alive with static on the
plastic slide. Across the street someone has
driven off the road, onto the sidewalk, halfway
through a boxwood hedge. Down the street
the arena, its stands ringing a small patch of
ice. Down another street my friend's favourite
breakfast place. Across from there my doctor's
office. My doctor who had six kids and the
youngest had childhood depression, too, she
said, pointing at a family picture taken at
Sears. Nearby was our middle school, which
later became loft apartments. Looming over
it, train tracks and a rocky point we called the
Peak, as if the world had only one. We were
picking the static girl up from camp, my friend
and I. It was the year someone took the "L" off
"Community Pool." Maybe a year my friend
was groped in passing, or maybe a year I was,
or both. In middle school, my best friend's
cousin reduced the French teacher to tears

and now someone touches their hand to the refurbished wood of their windowsill. People visited our town on the weekends because there was a natural-food store whose name recalled Biblical plenty. Archways into the alleys where the horses used to be kept. A bookseller who rescued orphaned raccoons. Waterfalls off this road and that. Down that street I got called one name for wrong gender and then another and a Frosty burst at my feet. Another time I was still the wrong gender but a man slowed his car down and told me all the things he'd do to make my wrong body his. A neighbour said *hop in* but I wanted to walk. The neighbour said *I won't bite!* My friend and I were picking the static girl up from camp and maybe it was a day where nothing went wrong and we ran through a sprinkler and spooned melon from its skin, walked her dog, got into only a safe kind of trouble.

When the forest burns, the bark of the trees
wards off the flames until it no longer can;
after that, the trees fall or stay standing. If they
burn hot, their roots go, too, and your foot
will sound a hole in the trail until your calf,
or thigh. After the fire, if you look up and see
green, the tree is still   alive. The spring
after the fire, when you think the fire is out, it
will have been smouldering over winter inside a
log or two, and it will come back. The fireweed
will arrive, and the ferns will unfurl from what
look like burned-out stumps. The fire will get
a little oxygen, it will remind everyone what it's
capable of, and then it will go out again.

NOTES

The transsexual empire has been coming like the Apocalypse
  "To fight *The Transsexual Empire*," University of California,
  Berkeley, professor Grace Lavery wrote in a since-deleted 2019
  Substack post, "is to become infected by its derangement." An
  earlier, much longer iteration of this poem engaged more deeply
  with the thinking in the trans-exclusive "feminist" book *The
  Transsexual Empire* in order to refute it and argue back. This
  iteration opted not to.

I keep returning to an essay about a rose garden
  Alexander Chee, "The Rosary," in *How to Write an Autobiograph-
  ical Novel: Essays* (Boston: Mariner Books, 2018).

Jamie Oliver shows American children
  Jamie Oliver's Food Revolution, season 1, episode 2, "Episode 102,"
  directed by Brian Smith, created by Jamie Oliver, aired March 26,
  2010, on ABC, abc.com/shows/jamie-olivers-food-revolution
  /episode-guide/season-01/02-episode-2.

On this map, a strip of pinkish-red
  US Central Intelligence Agency, "Standard Time Zones of the
  World," uploaded by TimeZonesBoy on Wikimedia Com-
  mons, accessed January 2023, commons.wikimedia.org/wiki
  /File:World_Time_Zones_Map.png.

the Vancouver episode of Art in the Twenty-First Century
  Art in the Twenty-First Century, season 8, episode 1, "Vancouver,"
  directed by Pamela Mason Wagner, created by Susan Dowling
  and Susan Sollins, aired September 23, 2016, on PBS, art21.org
  /watch/art-in-the-twenty-first-century/s8/vancouver/.

In the fall of 1999, at the age of thirty-five
  This line is adapted from Ann Patchett, *Truth & Beauty: A
  Friendship* (New York: Harper Perennial, 2004), 185.

Gone are the days of dawdling
  This line comes directly from Kayla Czaga, "Gone Is the VHS.
  Gone Is the Whir.," in *For Your Safety Please Hold On* (Gibsons,
  BC: Nightwood Editions, 2014), 54.

my favourite Ginsberg poem
  Allen Ginsberg, "Love Poem on Theme by Whitman," also
  known as "Epithalamion," first published in *Reality Sandwiches*
  (San Francisco: City Lights Publishers, 1963). The poem begins,
  "I'll go into the bedroom silently and lie down between the
  bridegroom and the bride ..."

ACKNOWLEDGMENTS

Previous versions of some of these poems were published by the *Malahat Review*, *This magazine*, *Grain*, *CV2*, *Fiddlehead*, *Arc*, *Room*, and *Poetry Is Dead*.

The writing of this book was supported by the Al Purdy A-frame Residency and the Conseil des arts et des lettres du Québec.

Thank you to Will, who helps me make space to write. Thank you to Kim and Ben. Thank you to Leah. Thank you to Michael, who left too soon and whose loss affected many. Special thanks to my editor, Catriona, and to Emily for her insights on this book in manuscript form. (I'm so sorry I forgot to warn you about the vomit, Emily.)

andrea bennett is a National Magazine Award–winning writer and editor who lives in Ayjoo mixw, BC. Their previous books include the poetry collection *Canoodlers* (Nightwood Editions) and the essay collection *Like a Boy but Not a Boy* (Arsenal Pulp Press), a 2021 American Library Association's Over the Rainbow longlist selection and a CBC Books pick for the top Canadian non-fiction of 2021. They co-host a *Great British Baking Show* rewatch podcast called *The Rough Puffs* with Kim Fu. Find them on Twitter at @akkabah and on Instagram at @andreakbennett.

PHOTO: ERIN FLEGG